Letters to the World

by

Jesus Rafael Weber

1. Do you?

Excuse me sir, where is salvation?

Where? By temptation? Oh, one

More thing. Just what will I

Need to meet the Supreme Being?

A soul? And love? And

Nothing more? Well then, will

He be free, to see me? But

I have a soul, and I

Know of love! And nothing more?

Oh! Now I see. What I

Don't yet feel. Yeah, I guess

It's hard. I know that part…

2. Raising our Hand To God

More than ever man has put

Himself in a position to act

As God in the Political, Medical,

Religious and Law branches of our combined

cultures. Although this trend

Is noticeable in Eastern Civilizations, the practices

In the West stand out like a

Sore thumb. Maybe this

Indirectly will bring about a Christian

Armageddon.

Sooner than its time. Never

The less anyone affiliated in some kind of

Religious Practice knows better than

To take the place of God

Yet we constantly place ourselves

In situations now; predicaments

Later, that will come to the end,

Go on our report cards.

Maybe fundamentalists are

Right in this commitment to

The Bible. In this day of

Age, death is cheap for the

Ailing. Who's to pull the plug?

Military power, nuclear power, Armageddon, or

Any form of power is limited, often concentrated to

one group? Or an individual. People

Die and kill for their beliefs, who's to

Say they're right? People are sentenced to death, do

we now have an artificial

Power to the hands and feet?

3. Ugly Little Slug:

An ugly little slug

May know time better

Than an ugly little

Human. (I have seen

In reoccurring dreams).

There is no such thing

As time, years, weeks

Or a calendar. Everything

Happens at once, but to

Us (minute little slugs

With egos, we see an everlasting

Day dragging on.) The truth

Is (in my dreams) we were

Born and dead at the same

Exact time. Just like an

Ugly little slug that doesn't

Seem to move, already did

Before it started. A "life"

Is but a sigh at a star.

(In my dream, oh how

Crazy they must be!)

4. I am:

I am subtle and hopeful

I wonder where your thoughts are

I hear a whisper in my mind

I see a sunrise in your eyes

I want a part of your heart

I am subtle and hopeful

I pretend to be unfeeling

I feel inane in your life

I touch a thorn to bring me back

I worry sick all night and day

I am subtle and hopeful

I am…I am…

5. Waste:

There's just waste of

Time in everything

I do, when my

Chair is boring

My bed is

Snoring. The window

Is fogging.

Get up, sit down

Get up, sit down

This room is going to

Heaven, now blow

It out, suck it in

Then out, my fingers

Yellow and

My cigarettes, are

Pulsing

Brown sugar is no

Consolation in my

Coffee anymore

Choke; choke,

They choke on

The worn tile

Floor. Change

The sneakers.

I'm staying in

Last night, tonight and

Tomorrow, since

Since you went away.

6. Violin:

A tear plucks the metal strings

The sound tears down my walls,

Where emotion bleeds and stings!

Some call a heart… what calls?

…the deepest part of me?

There's no thing as: Liberty!

Rotten, stinking cedar wood…

Feverish music kills my mood!

Fingers of lighting…don't know

They convert to madness!

The figure…same? I'd say no…

Beats wood? That answers kindness?

But! Applause, applause.. said!

With tears…was how I paid.

7. Who is:

(who is her? God is her and him and us and them!)

Once in a while I catch sweet glimpses

Of her face

But that was all

Then again she speaks a passing

Word of friendship

But that was all

And when I think I hear her

Loving voice upon me, that is all

And nothing more...

Once in a while I could look to her

And say

"This is all..."

Sometimes I would turn to smile at her,

So she could see..

Then again my words are shy and

Deeply troubled,

To say I...

And when I hear her voice again

Maybe

I may...

8. Understand:

Understand where you are

And where you are going

Realize your feet on the ground

And your head upside down

In your space you call a life

Lives the meaning of your existence, and

In mine and his and hers

Where there is life there is…

Understand a breath of life

Is a breath of love

A breath of love is a wind of…

Understand, please understand

Where you stand and where you were standing…

9. 23:44

There are times

And then there are times

I wish would not happen…

What is the purpose

Of solitude?

Of Loneliness

I ask?

But no answer.

Just Quiet. Quite like

Yesterday and the days

Before, I ASK?

I pray

I shout out loud

For the light

From God above

Are you there

Have you forgotten

Or have i…

I think the latter

My development

Is not complete

I have not

Reached my

Epiphany.

Leave and Stay.

10.   22:49

There is a small place in Gilroy

A small room,

A Big Heart

A suffering Romantic

Why is this the price I

Pay for thinking

Good,

For giving

In to the will above

To the word of…

I feel forsaken here on Earth

In this dimension, in this body

Move and ruled by

The directions in my Head

Ha, aha, yes

In my head there are

Directories and then

Some more

Sub, and sub and

While the galaxies await

& my light

My development

My cocoon to

Shed, so I

May light this

World away

...the development

The struggle the ever changing

Light, that is ALL

ALL we are, some more

Than others, others more...

But they don't know It.

11. I am, therefore:

I am therefore I will be

Light again. My time here is

Expired, my meter due

In the red. I do not want to borrow one more

Minute here on land, by 7 seas

In this atmosphere. I no longer want to contribute

And go in circles endlessly.

Take me now, set me free

I beg of thee, in the quiet

Hours let me be, the way

I have to be.

Then a bee flies on a flower,

That is development, pure artistry...

When a man, is too depressed, when his heart

Beating loudly, is not heard, he could not even

Compete with the little bee's deed. So I say

Again, let me be

Be light, let me go in peace

And leave peace for others

That know me as I am.

12. What I want:

There are no more letters for me to write, there are

no more words that seem just right. I have guided

my fingers to do my mouth's loudest will, but the

words I mutter have grown still.

Still I do not wonder or really care, when I think

about the final stair.

Stair way to freedom, steps to release, fear and

depression.

What I want?

A warm hand

A soft heart

Passion

Intensity

A quiet moment

Shared…

Not alone but

Shared quietly

With another, exquisite

Entity.

Nonsense!

It was not real on that hill, that mountain, the

eagle…the sky…the stars…the thunder…the

light…the struggle…am I really the translator or a

messed up prophet?

13. Letters to the World I:

…before we begin, a few notes from the author: "I

write about things I experience, things that anger

me or inspire me….Nothing but the old 'Sunday

Funnies.'

"I don't consider myself to be a poet, I just want to

be heard. Just like a baby cries for urgency; there is

an urgency, perhaps perseverance in my soul that

needs to be heard, criticized or maybe even exploited."

"My inspiration is Nature, or should I say natural? Nevertheless, my young, inexperienced 'works' are raw and simple. My drive comes from my experiences in this fast paced, quick kill sort of world we live."

"Call it what you'd call it anyways...Me? Why I call it a world sewer that overflowed onto my paper."

...and now we begin:

14. A.T.S.:

The little boy would sit and watch her for hours, at a time. He wondered where she could be. He knew better than to think she was only sleeping. No, there was more than that, and only a boy his age could really understand.

Ais, Ais he would whisper out loud, every time he made a wish. Slowly Ais would twitch her beautiful serene head, between the snow white ears. With a wink of her eyes she'd look up to the boy and "purr". The boy of ten, wondered about Ais, mostly when Ais left him, leaving him only to stare and wait for her return. One day he'd too leave with Ais, somewhere far away. He too would close his eyes, leaving behind the playground, the cruel children whom teased, his troubled parents and that cold, menacing look from the teacher. The more he watched Ais, the more he longed to be with her. Close…closer than he could here in his room, closer even than when he and Ais would hide around the giant golden wheat fields.

One night the little boy awoke to find Ais at his side. He looked deep into the bright red eyes, further than ever before. There were no distractions now, not even the ghost of the night or a thin breeze of air.

Nothing could touch him now...there were no lights, there were no dreams, there were no thoughts or worries, not even impossible questions to be answered. Inside of "Air" he saw more than he'd ever seen before. And for the first time in his short life, the boy was happy. The smile on his face gave it away, his wish had come true. Ais had found a home for him.

...and as the boy looked back, he saw "them" crying...he wondered...why?

15. Faith:

Last night I looked
To the North Star in question.
I prayed for a sign
From a falling star,
In patience.
The star did not fall,
But my question was answered in a

Restless sleep.

I woke up today, didn't

Know where I had been.

My mind wandered into

The desert windstorm

In a daydream state.

Tonight after a long

Thought out day, I prayed

After, first not being

Able to gaze (for shame) up to the

Stars, illuminating the

Desert sky. Once I found

Courage and fell

On my faith, I felt

At ease as my

Eyes fixedly gazed,

At the Milky Way stars...

16. TOLL to Soul:

...take my hand now,

Let me lead you through my mind

And guide you to my soul

Compassion, passion, tears and fear...

The gate ahead knows no exit

Do you walk upon my cobblestones?

It's cold in here (I know)...

My past has made it so.

I need a keeper to the Inn,

That is my soul

Thoughts and words won't even matter

As you often lead me into a fountain of laughter...

I'm anxious to lead you in...

But the cost is your Heart and Spirit

If you answer...

17. Mother Earth:

So the Earth trembles

Not for destruction...

But for respect.

How long have we exhausted

Scarred and condemned the

Ground below us? As

Far as man can see, he

Is on top, standing proud

And victorious. Master of

The soil and it's treasures.

Yet the Earth is our Mother…

That feeds and protects us…

Shelters and provides…

Much too often towards our:

Selfish, greedy, arrogant, materialistic

Needs, of excessive pleasure,

When we go too far…one day…

The Earth will turn us around and man will

Witness…crying out…

As the Earth, "Below", us

Turns us around.

Until we are floating on thin air

With no foundation at all. The Earth is and will

All ways will be on top. It is

Out of pity, that we stand on

Solid soil now...

18. Choice:

If death be all that life be not:

Then is death like a bird in flight?

Ready to stop if it were not for it's

Will and instincts to go on...

Why then, death must feed on the

Weak at heart, the lost in soul and

The failures in faith. Is life a parallel

Between continuity and death. How

Does one cross the line then? If by

Chance he does fall into the realm of existence and

forever lives in eternity

How can he reach true death. Unless

Death dies as humans and animals seem

To die before helpless eyes. Hypocritical

People blundering over the loss of their

"Loved" one, why couldn't they have

Saved their souls sooner. Now death takes it's Toll

on earth. But man has one last choice

Between continuity and/or death. Death,

Which eventually will cease to exist for:

That when the cannibal no longer has

Flesh to feed on, he will eventually

Feed on himself. So be it...

19. Hard To See:

It seems hard for me to

Sympathize with a person

Like me.

I try not to let color,

Race and type to handicap your

Words.

It's hard to see, how close you

Are like me. All the things you

Do, I do too. I didn't know you

Could feel the way I do.

It's hard for me to

See, just how neat a person

You can be. I guess it's

Like "they" say, "The hardest person

To see is me…"

20.   Departure in the Night:

Bird of flight, don't

Leave tonight. The dew

In this night…

It would weigh down

Your flight. Could

You leave another day…

With a moon beam

As your light?

The business at hand

Is pressing (I know)

Could it wait...

But could it wait.

21. Call to Murder:

The world needs a resolution

Except a few in charge won't

Give in to a solution

A vast majority...usurped

By a corrupt minority. And now

It's time to face Armageddon,

The stars, the seas, sands...it's

All over for a hundred thousand

Mortal men. Listen to their voices carry,

Voices carry in the winds, as

They fade away into a hole of

Sand, into a meaningless blood

Red realm of nonexistence.

Again and again the guns go

Off, again and again pay the

Price. Who pays the price?

And dies...who waits and

Cries. And it's the innocent

Who die in Mass.

22. Awake

If I have ever waited for

Something to happen...

Not this. I run into

A forest, looking for a

Compromise, then my mind

Is filled up with bullets

And mines. Now I am awake.

I'm awake.

23. The Bible:

Who is ready to read the Bible?

Read in fear. The Bible,

The good reward...evil stifle!

Turn one page at a time; forget...

Not...Or soul subject to regret,

The wrath in heavens while they wait,

Neglect will make the Spirit faint...

Words that hold on history...embedded

In the Scriptures. Left un-cremated...

Clearing way for man to follow...

Faith-no-more will keep one hollow.

Turn, obey, just plead forgiveness...

And true hearts see God not merciless.

24. Black:

...Hidden deep beneath

The surface, black thoughts

Black feelings, lurk abundantly

Often contained within, but never

Usurped totally, by anyone or

Anything. In the moments

You are too ashamed to look

Up to the skies, the black hold, holds

Your head down low, dark and gloomy

Like a rain cloud. When you

Want to give but take instead,

Your heart breaks at your

Lover's high expense. Black in darkness,

You can't see, when your mind

And soul are so colored viciously.

When anger creeps inside your bones, it's

No use to try and fight…surrender…

The black abyss is in control.

25. How?:

One of the most frightening

Experiences for me has been the

Constant repeat of the word

HOW?

HOW...how...how?

Not bad, huh? Well look at

It this way. STOP immediately

And touch yourself anywhere.

Or just touch anything,

Try to see yourself standing

On air, maybe in space.

HOW? How is it you are here?

Of course you were

Born and all. But how?

I don't mean the art of sex.

But the act of creation...

How? Is science a coup out? And religion

A stabilizer? How are

People walking, how am I and you

So small compared to what is outside this little

planet.

Think.

Close your eyes and

See yourself, where? Anywhere? How

Do you do that? Evolution?

Big Bang? How did anything get there?

How do I work? How is the meaning of life?

HOW?

26. Still waters run deep:

The pool of water is so clear, still I often

Find it hard to see bottom where there is none. I

imagine one

Up in my mind so I won't drown in a helpless

confusion. And if I falter in a splash, will the water

hold my pain…or

The weight of my fear and anxiety. Or will my end

be deep beneath the clear pool of water where no one

will ever hear

Me. Choke me now in shallow waters where my

body will wash

Ashore. 'Cause in the deep my corpse won't float with a rock

Tied unto my soul…and I often wonder how can a pool of

Water be so deep inside of me…

27. Mystery:

Take my mystery to bed

Why don't you

If Romance is what you need

Share with me

I'm going crazy with foreign ones

Help me!

The sky is falling over, and the

Peer pressure keeps

Building on.

I don't care for it if you don't

And I won't say it…if you don't…

Why do we play these games again,

Do you feel the urge…

Then take my mystery to bed…

28.   The eye of the storm:

In the eve of the morning

There is one mourning…

A man whose trust has

Been lost, caught in the

Middle he's violently tossed…

The eye of the storm sees

All situations, but lacks

In hearing late considerations.

There is something to be

Learned, as the man's

Faith had turned…

Anyone can be carried

Away in his own perseverance,

Which can often account for

The man's disappearance.

As the elements gain their powers,

The man's pain now towers...

He'd had the chance once,

Now his word amounts to an ounce...

And in his last hours here

Is his story...

A man lost in quest...

To gain glory...

He wanted much more than

He'd give...

But the woman he loved

Wouldn't live...

With is selfish approach,

This caused her to leave...

There was a chance once,

When he came to his senses...

But the man was young,

Took advantage of chances...

That the lady gave to him

Over and over…

But the man had a weakness so now it is

Over…and over…

Again he wishes he'd

Had courage or foresight

And the clear eyes

From age…and…and

If only he had one more little chance…

…The storm closes in on

The shores of its victim.

And now he realizes his

Confidence tricked him.

His last thoughts whistled

Away as the storm gained

Momentum. And they circled

Around him as to torment him…

The raindrops were falling.

Sprinkling his heart all over

New land…over

Places where others held

Up their hand...

...And realizing the rain

Was a hazard they took

Umbrellas to block the man's tears...

For the loss of a man's love

Is always his own, and

The weight that this carries

Comes always along.

29. Fire! In my cell!

Inferno fire of the macabre

Consuming anything to heave

Your destruction. Dancing

Wildly you mesmerize

Furious helpless eyes. Glowing!

Roaring! Virtuoso un-matched

By any earthly thing. Play...

Play and dance! All at once

In fulfilling satisfaction

Smolder and excrete unearthly

Gases!

"Prisoner in a cell...your

Hope was in a well. Not

Here.

Not

Here."

30. Portent #3:

The weather

Is

Warmer than before

The air

Is

Thinner than my hair.

Breathing

Is

Like smoking harsh Tobacco

I get dizzy just from sleeping.

But am I upset?

No! I couldn't

Be…I work tomorrow…

31.   Art:

I saw a woman in an art gallery.

But she did not speak.

I asked a hundred times,

But…I did not speak.

She held a basket full of fruit,

…too green to eat.

This woman I noticed was alone

In the world, she has a

Necklace full of pearls.

This woman stood high

Above me…

I only stared and thought,

What type of man would marry this woman?

This virgin woman who didn't speak,

What a world.

If she held her looks…

But lost the pearls…

If she smiled more…

If she held a basket full of ripe fruit

Instead…then I could ask a hundred times again.

32.   Mother:

Oh mother you are in need

Sick and tired

Frayed by age

Still I sit deep in thought

Unable or willing to adhere

To your aid! What type of

Son have you labored and

Pained? Who can't come

At once to his mother's aid?

I want to be there but

It's so much easier to stay

Hidden in excuses of time

And Distance. One day

I may fall dead on my

Prevailing thoughts for it

May be too late for any

Second Thought.

Your son.

33. Dreams:

Infinite Dreams take no time at all

A dream as I believe

But many others don't.

Is the closest thing

To real reality I know.

Why, I stagger all day,

Working, playing, talking

Into ends. In

My dreams, I'm heard,

For eons and then some.

Dream…dreams get me close…

To the furthest

Place I'm capable of dreaming of.

34.   The Run:

I do not need legs to

Remember what has been

Nor a heart, for my mind

Is above all that. I am

  The quiet competitor

Against time and man.

My face is like an old

Sponge, my lungs create the

Cavity of a mushroom,

My heart is like a bad check,

Due with interest. I don't speak

To no one, because no one

Knows what it was like to

Have it all then let it go
Slowly everyday. The only
Consolation is knowing I was
There and could have grabbed
It, instead I would never
Kick the habit.

35. Silent as the rose:
Hold on to the silence
You bestow upon the air
Surrounding your graceful
Steps. It is I who holds
His breath indefinitely
In the presence of your
Beauty. Silent as the rose
You open up the petals to
Your heart and leave a trail
I wouldn't miss in my most selfish
Moment. Your soul in ceaseless vigil

Goes, you ever so silent as the rose,

Leaving the loudest most audible impression

Upon me.

36. Yesterday:
(To God. It is hard not to question destiny

sometimes…)

They say good things never last,

One day you are happy, might

Be your last.

They say good things never last,

One day you found love, next day

It's…Past.

I wish that life were never ending…

All the good things, they are not sending…

They say all good things never last,

One day you're happy…Next day…

Is your last…

37. Priest:

I can no longer be my self

My conscience will no

Longer tolerate my present

Precious lifestyle

My skin is shedding

A new leaf is turning

I must accept now

Unconditionally what I have

Always been

But have not summoned

My mind is almost ready

For what my conscience has

Always been waiting

For.

38. Thought:

I wish I had the light to see,

All the things you do for me…

Behind my back, when I'm asleep,

You often conceal your deeds from me.

No one else could understand the

Language between us. Or the continuity

In our thoughts.

39. Words:

Truth is an opinion

Either yours or someone

Else's

Faith is a security

Either real or outspoken.

Communication is so self-centered

Always to obtain.

Knowledge, serious, stern, sour,

Like the medicine it is…

For ignorance…

40. Justice:

Justice to make right

To avenge, for revenge?

Justice from freedom

To imprison, to extinguish?

Justice a practice of

Law and order where

Is the origin? Is

Justice the result of experience, good versus bad…

In weight. Justice

Is to morality as a mind is to a heart…

The two can't work together…

41. Universal Waste Disposal:

Earth is just a great big

Tombstone and life here is the

Last funeral…If we have

Wars, let's have them here.

Saving our own planets…

We will invent weapons, we will

Spread hunger, torture the
Weak, dump nuclear waste,
Poison the skies, ravage
The forests, dry up the oceans.
Yes! Yes!...this
Planet Earth will welcome destruction,
Saving our own kind. When we leave
For home, it will all
Be out of our system...
Left to linger back on Earth.
How will they welcome it!

42. The broken bottle:
That broken bottle was for me!
I was not skilled in fixing glass.
But then one day it came at last.
I fixed the bottle, re-shaped the sides,
Now, that broken bottle is fixed at last.

43. John:

I've seen this picture a million times!

Could it be my mistake?

Could I have missed this very portrait?

Just a kid, who committed ruthless crimes…

I see a young man, who sees the light…

Who has taken a different path, 'could this be right?

He walks along, he might be wrong, he walks

along…

But not alone, the path he's taken will be long…

But before…I saw the scenery,

A wanted life, a wasted life.

A dirty place, a dirty jail, a fruitless life,

And damning crimes.

I don't understand, the scene has changed…

He wears the Robes, and has been saved.

44. My Romance is…

Balanced perfectly…

With an arrogant attitude,

Sometimes…

She is lady like,

With a fine-boned fragility.

Romance-delicate,

Possessing a Tragic sensuality,

Inner strength fueled by

Twitchy intensity…

Magic surrounds her in…

An air of sophistication

Genuine Warmth glows

Like an aura within her.

Large loud and proud…

This body communicates

To all heads that turn…

With pride and conviction…

Her love is

Variety…

Long, long legs

Complimented by

Those impossible curbs

Generate sexual electricity…

Improbable lips,

A lower lip at half mast

Turns to a smile…

My romance is…

Charm…

Other men after her

Flew…but

Her card was in

My destiny

Now…

This Angel-fun girl

Defines

Beauty

And there was

Passion about

When i… she Seduced…

45.   A place inside your heart:

…At that time a great city,

With a cosmopolitan population

And an apparently well deserved

Reputation for immortality

In my young eyes. Not long

After the departure, it appears

That some members of this

Splendid city, fell back into

The evil ways of the place, and

Although many wrote and asked

Advice, the reply was misunderstood

And quickly forgotten. And me?

I had no choice but to flee in haste,

Which later turned to a bitter and

Sorrow anger. However I will never…

Ever see, but the city walls of this Place inside your

heart.

46. Don't feed an open window:

When the wind starts calling out

Through the open window. Rush

To shut it, don't look out! Keep

Passing the open windows…

That's all you can do in life…unless

Of course the ground right under

You gives way and you feel

You're falling. Maybe then the

Inclination to jump may lead you…

…At this moment weigh the

Future…and pass the open window.

47. Take two minutes:

Take two

Take two minutes

Every morning

To come to grips

With whom you are now.

Take two Carnations

Every evening

To help you sleep

With a dream of grace.

Make two wishes

Every evening

To come true soon

With stars as witnesses.

Make two promises

Every morning

To fulfill with sincerity

With a heart of liberty.

But most important

Every evening

Take two Carnations

To give thanks above

For the individual you are.

48. Just Do it:

Knowledge

Awareness

2 steps to

Success

For a race

Of people

Called inferior, less.

Competing today

Would not be

So hard

If only I

Had a set of white hands.

Meaning to speak

Out, the cat

Hid away my

Tongue

My place in the spectrum

Is way below

Yellow.

Black Thursday…

Black Monday…

Black Magic…

Black Cat, bad

Luck.

Why do they

Always

Notice the

Color first?

49.   A soldier's tale:

Where gentle hills were green with trails…

An old man sits and tells a tale.

His hair is grey, his bones now creak…

This man has been long extinct.

"A seed was planted, a flower bloomed…

That flower is under a million tombs."

"Where crystal clear rivers once had ran…

Where erosion came and made them damned."

"Where birds once sung with tunes so gay…

Now stands a carcass, from ruthless play."

"Where churches rand their morning bells…

But why? Now there's hell; the story tells."

"Don't leave me now, comrade. I cry to you…

Oh, please believe me I'd die for you."

That man won't move, he sits and waits.

His brain is dead, the world he hates.

He'll sit now, lost in time.

Remembering his evil crime.

50. Spit on a Windshield:

Who's world is it really?

I mean… We claim any Land

We can, through war

Or exploration. I wonder

If someone, or something (s), have

Claimed us? One day to come

And say, "Get out. We claimed

This part of the Solar System

And we're here to colonize, and

Make you our slaves."

Could this thought be so far fetched? I mean

We know now that our Solar System

Is not the center of the Universe-

But just dust blowing around...

There is evidence of other Solar Systems

And Planets. Would it be an

Evil twist for the "superior" races of the

World, to be slaves to another

World? Whom would adjust the best...

... who would want to?

51. Hold, on Paper:

Hold, on Paper

For those whose hearts

And lives are on

Paper- There's the risk

Of total fire. There's

No cure for those who

Paper their souls. I

Pray someone one day

Will free mine...

52. New Year:

This year I'm making

One sole resolution because

Two are hard to keep.

The precedent months,

Weeks and days have

Taught me a lesson that

Will forever scar my

Values. That lesson

Now embedded in my mind

Is about human feelings

And love. Never again

Will I linger in my

Own selfish needs at the

Expense of my love. That

Is to: love my self as much

As I love others I really

Care about. When I do

Things that I always

Meant to happen will.

This will be risky

And most probable

With it's hardships, because when

You are shooting for a star

There is a long way to fall.

53. Closet:

the door is shut and

I'm sitting by the corner

I hope someone will

open the closet door

why?

so I can tell them to

leave me alone-

go away!

with each passing moment, I'm

sitting in the corner

why don't they open

the closet door?

54. Balance:

Trying to balance this

cigarette on the edge

of this coffee cup has

been impossible. I

try and try again.

Will I ever learn?

I hope… Maybe

one day, if there's

any left in the pack-

I'll try balancing

one out, that isn't

lighted.

55.   Bizarre Dream:

Have you ever felt the air?

Or seen limit to the sky?

Would it be so far fetched-

to say… Well, you see here

an Universe, can't see us (too small)

But if you were

by some bleak chance (wouldn't, but),

Outside, Well, I feel

you would say, "There's

truth in the bean stalk!

See the Jolly Green Giant…"

56. Disguise:

I wonder if this tree cleverly

disguises itself: with thorns

or wilting leaves. Maybe
this tree is smiling inside
while the fruit it bears is
rotting outside. How could
this tree still stand tall?
When the branches break and
the leaves are dead? I
have no time for dying
trees! So I walk away-
and as I do, I wonder
if that's exactly what the tree
wants me to do.

57. Iraq:
A night in Iraq
A blanket of fog covers
the vast sea of sand
packed down by a surprisingly
Heavy rainfall

I see a half bright moon,

Straining to see the other

Mysterious shadowy half.

The night complimented with

Silence and darkness whispers to me,

Relaxes my state of being

With the exception of

the distant sounds from

Generators and the ritualistic

Barking and yelping from a pack

of wild dogs, this

night's silence sits heavy

in my heart.

I look up and wonder…

I gaze into the night in

admiration, fear and frustration…

My thoughts blowing away with each

exhale of smoke from my lungs.

Still I wonder…

Not very far into this night

Not very deep under a heavy grey Blanket

Of fog, the souls of thousands sleep.

and whisper around me-

know their angry smells from

the hot days-when the

wind blows skyward-

This is when I look around and see if the acrid

smoldering scents

are not actually from burning…

a burning pot of feces

and when I can't spot a fire ignited-

anywhere…

I wonder. If they can understand me,

if they can break a language barrier

see inside my heart-

how very sorry I am,

how much I wish

to have been someone

who could had made a

difference…

and when I look into

the Night-

then gaze back upon the half Moon

I wonder…

I can hear their voices

I can hear their curses…

Iraq.

…their muffled voices from under the

ground, screaming out into this

very night…

to the pack of wild dogs, commanding them

to curse and haunt us in our camp.

Black dogs, angry dogs howling

with pain, barking with laughter,

keeping us nervous for their masters-

when I hear them from a distance-

when I see the emissaries staring at me-with smoldering hollow eyes during the day.

I wonder... I really do...

58. My Theory:

I predict we all are a part of you and you a

part of me. Except when atoms split, if the case may

be. A

stone a tree might be a bee. I am an atom, why me?

Mass

can't be lost like energy. But one's should sure can

be. I

may live or leave. The choice is mine, it's up to me.

59. ??:

Growing in Sin to Armageddon

When I stabbed you in the back,

or when I hit you with my car.

How did you feel, I don't care.

Did you taste the bitter in your

drink? It was poisoned. When

you slept, I brought you nightmares.

There's six bullet holes in

your jacket; the blood

stains in your Sunday shirts never

wash away. What were you

expecting? I sent you six black

roses. I've brought disease,

your loved ones now deceased. Through

it all, and through it all, you are still faithful.

You still listen, and you

go on pleasing me. Sorts like

you will never learn, reach

for your pockets full of worms.

You're the type I need, when the last day

comes along. Your name bears

substantial numerical value

in my throne. When the bottle

comes, may I be

victorious at Armageddon

As long as you come back

for nothing, time and time again.

I will take the place of Popes, I will be

"Vicarious filii dei"

And who is there to stop me?

Sincerely, Master Satan…

60. Smoke:

Does the light burn only by the effort of its master,

or

does it sometimes have a will of its own that keeps

the time

running for only three minutes, three months, three

decades.

To the butt every time; even the most persistent can

only

force the filter to char for only a few seconds. Why

does

it appear many lives parallel a trail of smoke, that is the

product of a slow burning? And all at once all is lost with

a puff...

61. One Second:
I am so sad and...
lost with passion-
let me just lay down,
now at this very trying
moment while it still
hurts and lingers in
the air

62. Star:
I have not forgotten, nor will I
ever erase the ecstasy shared in our
embrace. In a place high above the

common city. Magic sensations

governed our gentle perceptions,

of the World below us and seas

floating in us. It's hard to be

regretful when there is a hand in

your hand. This is how…

This is our… This will be…

Our time.

Pausing shortly, gazing fixedly

upon the sky above us. Reaching

a point of ultimate immunity

to Worldly distractions. We

transcended and I know you

were there, because I kissed you

there - six-million miles ago upon

the star which we call ours to hold

forever.

63. No Other End:

A silent scream, inside of me

A mere twitch is all you'll see

Your face is blue your eyes are red

A mind you set and now have made

No turning back, at last you see

The time has come for you and me

A foreign land, so far away

My tears are gone, where trees now sway

I call to you, so far away

It's no use, your mind is set

To shoot and kill

your self this day.

64. Questions:

... The time at hand is a trying time

but the future holds a challenge

faith and trust in the things we

love- can and will overcome

the obstacles of time, distance

and temptation. Believe in who

you are and where I am…

Right there- the voice inside

your heart…

"I just want you to stop and think,

about something you

think about every day."

65. Sacred Land:

Many miles ago

There is the land

That drops and

Rises critically

It is not the land

for men and

their machines

Although Nature

warns off man

from his destruction-

The elements

have not been

enough to deter

man, from scarring

up the sacred land.

66. Candle Light Dream:

Ever light up a candle in a

Church? I would if I cared

what-so-ever, about the Sun, Seas,

and my Mercedes Benz. See

it this way: Know when

you think something, do something

for that thought, it always seems

to carry in the air? Well-

like a candle (again), hope

GOD's Angels don't forget to light

ours one day...

74

67. I Want To Be A Care Free Rain Drop:

I want to be a care free rain drop
dropping to the ground. Gently
falling if you like me. but
if you don't, take out a good
umbrella. I want to be a
care free rain drop-
Dropping while you sleep.
Cleaning up the houses
and any dirty streets. Listen
to me in friendly curiosity or
I'll drop on your head, to torture
you. One drop at a time. I want
to be a care free rain drop,
and wash away your dreams.
You won't need them…'cause
tomorrow you'll be drinking me.

68. Letters to the World:

Letters to the World, one at a time…

making sentences and words rhyme,

Letters to the World, from the inspector

of all time…

And every letter you have read before is a waste of

time…

Letters to the World, to let you know what to

expect,

when the clocks turn over in Y2K,

In 1999 I wrote this book,

but it took a future until I was no longer

misunderstood,

Letters to the World, are a collection of letters to

words that make up sentences, nouns, adjectives and

verbs…

Letters to the World, about a little bit of what is

wrong today…

Letters to the World, I hope one day someone reads mine someday…

69.   October:

I believe if you knew why my
tears fall so often
you could join me in an
Embrace, 'cause Winter kills
and it's just fall. Somewhere
In the forest there is a place
for me to rest fully outstretched
with folded hands upon
My breast. This fall my
slumber will be permanent and
I will smile. So wide and
Big, I may persuade black
Birds to sing. Somewhere in
October the ground is softer
Than in December. I will

Sleep then at the height of

My enlightenment. sleep…yes.

But not in vain, my body

will rest upon the copper-tone,

Fertile carpet of October, and

Be covered unsuccessfully

By the deceiving flakes of

December.

70. See the Fish inside me:

"Hello! Ho there- is anybody home? Hello-Well,

well, how do you do, young lad?"

"Fine thank you sir."

"Is mom or dad home?"

"No…no, but you can come in and see my fish

collection!"

"Well! That's quite a generous offer there…ah,

ah…"

"Ricky! My name is Ricky."

"Ricky? Yes, Ricky, I'll join you, but will your parents be home soon? I had several calls down at the

station. Neighbors complaining of funny noises and screaming. Everything seems fine here. Any problems Ricky?"

"No Sir. Everything is fine. Look! Look there, it's Mr. Bossol"

"Mr. Bossol? Ha! You named that little fish after Mr. Bossol? Quite a friendly old man I do say. Haven't seen

him since last week."

"And here is Betsy Rogers, and little Amy and…"

"Hey, you named all your fish after the whole town! Quite

a compliment! Is there one with my name?"

"No…no, Mr. Finch, not yet…Would you like to be?"

71.   This World is a Mess:

This world is upside down…

the words of hate are all around,

I cannot find the words to fix it,

I cannot find the time to mix it,

This world is upside down…

the words of men are missed and slandered,

as boys and toys showboat every hoax,

I cannot find the words to fix it,

I cannot find the time to mix it…

72.   The Time is Now:

The time at hand is now and pressing,

there is no time for courts and messing,

I know you know what everybody wants,

I know you know what everybody haunts,

Lucidity in my actions, and lucidity in my
compromises, I take flight on every instance of
infringement on human decency,
There is the great drugs of the Nations,
There are great kids dancing to the mushrooms of
the times,
while work and responsibilities take a back seat to
the dance-floors of weirdness and comatose feelings,
no body wants to work, nobody wants to raise a
child,
to live without a purpose and to drug your life away
with no time, no dates is what alienates all of us
from the time of all times, from the water of all
waters, from the light of all lights, and in the end no
body goes to mass anymore...

73. If I could only live again:
I have lived before...
You have died before...

Will you die again or will you carry carnations in
your hands instead of daisies from muddied slandered
public waters?
Do you know they are starting to holler,
news and signs of the times are on the streets as
colors rule every spectrum and people fight not
because they are lonely anymore but because they are
bored with blaming just themselves…

74. I do not know anymore:
I do not care…
I do not wish…
I do not know anymore what it was we started
along time ago, caught in traffic jams and airport
securities…
Why has it come to this?
There is always one apple that ruins it for the whole
bunch, and those apples must be not only plucked
first from the mainstream but from every society…

75. If you care to listen:

If you care to listen you will hear a sparrow a blue
jay and a songbird tweet and twitter about the
morning and the afternoon, if you care and listen you
will hear flat trees tell stories about ten different
angles on one truth…

Do you still care then? Do you still listen then? Or
do you demand a new song of truth and solidarity
with what is the only way something actually
happened without the opinions of celebrity birds?

76. Do you want to change:

Do you want to change?

Do you want to stay the same?

Do you want to spend some time away from me?

I will not beg you to hear my stories when you
know I have not always been alone, and I have not
always been away…

You must accept we both have histories and they included our pasts, and our pasts included friends and friends of friends and more than that…

If you cannot live by these truths then we cannot really be together from this point…So we must not linger in jealousy…

77. I am not jealous if you are not:

I have been to big cities…

I have been to big plays…

I have been to big concerts…

It does not mean I can't do it again with my present future…Can't I… Or will you make all the rules again?

78. If there is candy in sweet water:

If there is candy in sweet water, then I am a child again…

If there is water in sweet flows then I am happy
again...
If I find a pond, a pool of water that just filled
upon undisturbed stones, then I can sing again...
I just need a hand in my hand.

79. I know:
I know what I am...
I know what I want...
I know what I need...
To smell a pink rose next to me every morning...
And to clip every thorn except the one...
That brings me back to reality...
Marriage is what keeps life real...
I need to make my self available again...

80. Three steps:
One step and you are two less...
Two steps and you are one less...

Three steps and you are one more step away from any goal…

81.   If lilies of the valley could sing:

If lilies of the valley could sing they would say,

"Today, yesterday and tomorrow have just started,"

and I would believe every bee…

and I would believe every bird…

I would feel every breeze and I would sing along

too…

Because yesterday led to today and tomorrow has

always already started I am clean and wise again,

I am new again and I am confident I will make

music, art and poetry again in every corner of every

willing soul…(that understands the depths of the

sea, the heights of the atmospheres and shades of the

color gray).

82. Don't give up:

There have been many times I wanted to give up

until there was a moment again where I didn't…

When I was weak I staggered and fell…

When I came to, I walked again and refreshed my

self with the water…

I can, I will, I can, I will, let's do this together…

Raising a family takes two…

83. If:

If every tree could talk they would gossip

endlessly…

If every tree could walk they would cause mayhem

and traffic…

Yet I wish I could hear the chatter from the

elders…

Yet I wish I could wait behind something that did

not give off the smokes of slow moving

smokestacks…

84. The Value:

The value is not dollars and cents...

The value is not awards and accolades...

The value of a life is worth more than the value of a valley...

And the value of a life is worth the caring of every home, and every other living soul...

The value of your life is the value of the heart of hearts...

85. Pain:

There is only one kind available...

There is only one kind admissible...

Pain is for the gym...and only for there...

I need to get back there again...

86. The Streets:

The streets of New York...

The streets of London…

The streets of LA…

They are all clean again…

Because there is sense in the minds of women and men…that the rush of every morning is faster than the rush of every moment wrapped around the arms of loving arms…

87. Don't be:

Don't be so shy to tell me what you need…

Don't be so shy to tell me what you want…

Don't be so shy to keep things hidden behind…

Don't be so stuck in a moment that hold you too deep inside…

88. May 7th, 1970:

The day I was born.

"7" the number I personally believe in my belief system is the number of GOD'S ANGELS.

Taurus is my birth sign: I am not just ruled by
Venus. I am not ruled at all except by the virtues of
a loving, caring, warm, happy, funny, smart lady, I
have yet to find. I am loyal, I do like nice things, I
do like all
kinds of food, I am steady and methodical, I am
stubborn sometimes and I do like my privacy.
Lilies of the Valley my birth flowers are beautiful
upside down tea cups, that to me symbolize the teas
I give to others as I am not selfish and I am not a
stranger as I like to show off my best of me...
Those are the symbols of my birthday...

89. There is something to learn:
There is something to learn everyday...
There is something to do every positive, careful, and
empathetic way...
I am a man full of rivers, mountains and skies...
I do not like any lies...

I am a man that knows right from wrong...

I rarely have heard this sung in a song...

If there was a poem to describe my feelings...

It has not been recorded yet.

90. No way back:

There is no way back to what we had...

There is no way back to what we shared...

There is no way back to get there...

I can look to you and say, there is a better place for

me and there is a better place for you...

Inside someone else's heart...

91. Why do you?:

Why do you come here?

And why do you stay?

There's no place like home, but still, you go away...

And if I knew you like I used to, I would say...

Don't waste another day...

92.   This land is ours:

This land is ours…

This place is ours…

We make the rules…

We live and thrive here without you…

This land is ours…

And no other place will do…

93.   You should have:

You should have gone away from all this…

You should have thrown out all the letters…

I did not mean to hold you back…

I was not holding your hands…

But you were riding on my back.

94. I cannot go on:

I cannot go on with so much uncertainty…

I cannot carry forward dreams and hopes…

I have landed heavy upon every floor I have walked

on, and I can fall no more…

I cannot go on…

95. The dark heart:

You have tossed and turned enough…

You have taught and learnt enough…

You have seen the clouds grow gray and dark…

You have failed to achieve greatness in any life…

Yet you have the darkest heart…

96. Rainbow:

After the rain comes a rainbow…

After the pain comes the colors in the skies…

After the losses come the reconciliation…

After you lose comes another chance…

97. I miss you:

I miss you both…

You are my flesh and blood...

I miss the laughter and the smiles...

I miss the days of play and diversity...

I miss you both...

Sons...

98. If:

If greatness could be achieved in one day...

It would be holy...

If greatness came any other way, than a long road

of practice and participation...

Then greatness wouldn't be great...

99. Bee:

If you were a bee...you would be the Queen all the

drones would call on...

100. I am:

I am the mail you get every Saturday afternoon...

I am the flower that blooms summers, springs, winters and falls…

I am the spring of water where the flow never ceases….

I am the clouds that bring you mist and light rain on a very hot day…

I am the moon that rises when the sun falls…

I am yours…

101. Long Road:

It's been a very long road…

I have built many bridges and I have crossed many more…

I have found love, and I have lost love many times before…

I have made promises, and kept all of them until I revised the ones nobody gave me reason to keep…

I am immortal in any existence, yet mortal in a simple world…

I have yet to find what I am looking for, and I have not even had the chances to find it…

I have one, the one, I believe in and trust…

Together we will get to that place that has evaded us, all because I made one mistake…

I underestimated the hits of reality…

102. Again:

Again, I see petals on the ground…

The trees will be naked soon, like us, like we are…

There is no better way to be so you won't be stolen from…

They can see everything, and anything we are or have, so don't get dressed…

And the petals keep falling down on the ground…

103. Anything:

Anything with sunshine is like anything with rain when you need it…

Anything with love is like anything with

hugs and kisses when you need them…

Anything with relationships is like anything with

happiness and friendships when you need them…

Anything with life is like anything with

sunshine, rain, love and relationships when you need

them…

104. Undone:

She came undone when I broke up with her…

She came undone when I told her about her sins…

She came undone when I wouldn't listen anymore…

She came undone when the lights went out and the

house got cold.

105. Seashells:

Seashells and I have them all…

Seashells on the basement floor.

Seashells that sit still on the floor…

Seashells that never ask for more.

I can't tell you what to do.

I can't force you to the truth.

I can't be with you anymore,

But I can leave forevermore.

106. The First:

The first touch was the closest one...

The first kiss was the loveliest one...

And I think about you all the time, as my body and

lips have gotten cold and blue.

I wonder all the time where all that time blew.

And I can't be who I was anymore because all

that remains is only our ghosts.

107. Just Stop:

Just stop holding my head.

Just stop climbing the stairs...

Just stop screaming my name.

Just stop getting ahead…

There is a time to come undone,

And there is a time to listen…

But both of us don't have time for any compromises

anymore.

108. Swam:

She swam away with her voice in her hands…

On the very last day of all our stands…

She could carry on; she could keep on crying…

I always knew she was lying.

109. Porcelain:

Skin light as fresh fallen snow,

On a green field of freezing grass,

There is a body of leaves and twigs,

That doesn't move, cause winter stings

And fall is falling behind the snow again,

With the frost and the latter date,

Comes the new season of her fate,

To be or not, with or without him or her,

She is porcelain in the snowy ground, lain…

Delay not, wait never, it is here and there is no

turning back words from summer and fall said…

Porcelain with a pink bow and white dress,

Lies the princess, porcelain…

110. Before:

Before the Milky Way got sweet,

You stole something from me…

I came here to get it back.

You thought I died and forgot,

I did not,

I am back to get it back.

And when you taste the sour of the

Cold and dark stars,

You will know,

What you left me with.

111. Pose:

Pose between two perfectly aligned soft pink-red
petals with dew drops between them…
Pose walking on moss and holding satin as you hold
your breath…
You are walking along a path I remember but have
not seen in a long while…
You have not been forgotten, as I have not
forgotten your beautiful words…

112. Low Life:

There is no way we can find the light to take us out
of the darkness…
Time has ran out for a race of revengeful, bigots and
greedy individuals…
This will all end with a mushroom without a
salad…
Or will there be intervention before all the buttons
race to the end?

113. Who are you:

Who are you to tell me you know it better?

Are you enlightened or omnipotent?

Who are you to say you are better?

So your pocket book is deeper and your connections

wider?

That is not enough to carry you after you rest but

not in peace I promise…

114. Let go:

Let go of your hate…then there is hope…

Let go of your greed…then there is hope…

Let go of your high horse…then there is hope…

Just let go of your complications that you say

simplify and explain all that is wrong, because you

really don't know…

115. Shallow:

I got caught up in the shallow,

When I was really sinking in clear still waters…

I could go on trying to save you,

But I never knew you are past all your problems…

Sinking with me in the clear still waters…

116. Never:

Never take anything for granted…

It is not free no matter how generously you received

it,

Be wise with it before you lose it,

Because heaven has turned dark cold and old…

Waiting for someone to reach it.

117. You can:

You can say it matters…

You can say it doesn't matter,

Because you stopped caring…

118. News:

All I see on the news is crime, theft, murder…

All I see on the news is war, refugees,

homelessness…

All I see on the news is drug abuse, corruption, and

greed…

There are over one thousand billionaires driving up

prices…

And all I see on the news is poverty, gun violence,

bigotry…

All I see on the news…

119. No:

I do not want to hear your excuses…

You all have had enough time to come to the right

conclusions…

It only takes a few good solutions…

I don't want to budge.

I don't want to bargain.

I am an ambassador for one great One, not many
Lost so called ones…
I will not forgive you again…
Stop, the madness now.
Stop, the genocide now.
Stop, the greed now.
Stop, the inequality now.
Stop, just stop, before the One on my call get's
started.

120. Stages of my life:
Stage One,
I am born.
I breathe.
I am loved.
Stage Two,
I feel.
I reciprocate.
I am wiser.

Stage Three,

I am old.

I am sick.

I am not waiting to die.

121. Trees:

GOD is the trunk that holds the branches, we the people are the leaves that hold the dances. Us and GOD root into the ground for water that remind us to live and conserve in dry seasons. We are all unique leaves however no two leaves are alike. We all have one place on the trees however each of us only deserves and needs one home otherwise we would not be used to ourselves and our neighbors.

122. Skies:

GOD is the atoms that hold the atoms however we are the skies that are blue and clear until we are in communion and share our rain over the land with a message of hope, growth and sustenance. Dark skies are a warning some times from afar to remind us to share our local blue skies with our distant clouds as well and to respect each other's spots in the skies even when the winds breezes us along.

123. If:

If a rose petal could match your intelligence...then you would be the whole garden...

About The Author:

Jesus Rafael Weber, AKA, JRW 21, is also a music producer. You can find out more about him at www.jrw21.com There you will find more about his music styles and where to find his music online or in stores. JRW 21 was born in Guadalajara, Jalisco, Mexico; however, adopted at the age of around ten years old and brought back to the states. He was Naturalized into the U.S.A. in the early 80's. He attended Paso Robles High School, ran X-Country, Track and DJ'd music.

Later JRW 21 joined the military and was deployed to Iraq. When he returned from the Army, he became a graduate of College of the Redwoods and Consumnes River College. He has been married twice and has two sons.

He now lives in California and is working on his next Abstract Poetry Book with some iambic meter poems as well. You can visit JRW 21 at www.jrw21poetry.com